101 Successful Networking Strategies

ERIC KRAMER

Course Technology PTR

A part of Cengage Learning

COURSE TECHNOLOGY
CENGAGE Learning‍

Australia, Brazil, Japan, Korea, Mexico, Singapore, Spain, United Kingdom, United States

COURSE TECHNOLOGY
CENGAGE Learning·

101 Successful Networking Strategies
Eric Kramer

Publisher and General Manager, Course Technology PTR:
Stacy L. Hiquet

Associate Director of Marketing:
Sarah Panella

Manager of Editorial Services:
Heather Talbot

Marketing Manager:
Mark Hughes

Senior Acquisitions Editor:
Mitzi Koontz

Project and Copy Editor:
Kate Shoup

Interior Layout:
Shawn Morningstar

Cover Designer:
Mike Tanamachi

Proofreader:
Sandi Wilson

Printed in the United States of America
1 2 3 4 5 6 13 12 11

For product information and technology assistance, contact us at
Cengage Learning Customer and Sales Support, 1-800-354-9706.

For permission to use material from this text or product, submit all requests online at **cengage.com/permissions.**

Further permissions questions can be e-mailed to **permissionrequest@cengage.com.**

All trademarks are the property of their respective owners.

Library of Congress Control Number: 2011920280
ISBN-13: 978-1-4354-5984-7
ISBN-10: 1-4354-5984-9

Course Technology, a part of Cengage Learning
20 Channel Center Street
Boston, MA 02210
USA

Cengage Learning is a leading provider of customized learning solutions with office locations around the globe, including Singapore, the United Kingdom, Australia, Mexico, Brazil, and Japan. Locate your local office at: **international.cengage.com/region.**

Cengage Learning products are represented in Canada by Nelson Education, Ltd.

For your lifelong learning solutions, visit **courseptr.com.**
Visit our corporate Web site at **cengage.com.**

This book is dedicated to Zachary, Jake, Jon, Paul, Amy, Catherine, and Lisa—all important parts of my personal network.

I also dedicate this book to the networkers who truly understand networking, and whose first question is, "How can I help you?"

About the Author

Eric Kramer is a "serial careerist," having held 10 jobs in six distinctly different careers. Eric knows networking!

Eric started his professional career as a clinical psychologist, has managerial experience in both large and small companies, has owned a software-development company, worked as an IT project manager, and sold large-scale mental-health–management software. Eric also worked as a career consultant and career-center manager with two of the country's largest job-transition firms. In these positions, Eric worked with hundreds of job seekers individually and in groups, helping them develop career visions, teaching them job-search skills, and coaching them through interviews.

In addition to this book, Eric has authored *101 Successful Interviewing Strategies*. He is identified as a recruiting thought leader by Kennedy Information, writes the *Interview Your Best* blog (http://employmentinterview.wordpress.com/), and tweets as Interview_Best. Eric also developed the iBest Interview Presentation, http://www.interviewbest.com, a presentation job candidates develop and bring to their interviews to communicate their fit with the job requirements, differentiate themselves, and win interviews. Eric is a frequent presenter at local and national conferences on the subjects of interview presentations, online identity optimization, and career management.

Eric earned a bachelor's degree in Psychology from the University of Hartford and a master's degree in Counseling Psychology from American University. He is certified in positive psychology coaching and is licensed as a psychologist in the state of Pennsylvania.

Contents

Part 1

Connecting with Others: The Basics 1

Part 2

Networking Attitude:
Authenticity and Positivity **19**

Part 3

Building Your Network:
Quality, Not Quantity...............................**41**

Table of Contents

Part 4

Networking Etiquette:
Be Responsible, Respectful, and Responsive 65

Part 5

Networking Techniques:
Network Like a Pro **77**

Part 6

Creating a Conversation:
Talking Points......................................**101**

Part 7

Networking to Find a Job:
Stay Positive.....................................**113**

Introduction

Networking is simply the art of building relationships—relationships with people with whom we exchange support, information, connections, ideas, and a sense of belonging.

I wrote this book to help you quickly learn easy strategies for networking success. *101 Successful Networking Strategies* is based on the principle that thinking enables behavior. In other words, doing the right things becomes far easier when you think the right thoughts. Each think/do strategy in this book will first suggest a way to think, then guide you about what to do.

After reading this book, you will find networking much easier and more comfortable. And as you become more comfortable, you will do even more networking, leading to even more life and career success.

Good luck with your networking.

Eric Kramer, M.Ed.

1

CONNECTING WITH OTHERS: THE BASICS

1.

Networking: It's Just Another Form of Social Connecting

What to Think

Networking is just a special form of social connecting. Although we use it to achieve something—for example, meeting somebody, learning something new, or finding a job—at its core, networking is about establishing a social connection and then using that connection to further your and the other person's goals.

What to Do

Apply the techniques of effective social interaction. If you are good at forming friendships and business relationships, you have all the skills required to be a good networker. Just take those same social skills and apply them to networking.

2.

Be Aware of Where You Are

What to Think

In social situations, both one–to-one and in groups, it is important to be able to predict the consequences of your behavior. In order to anticipate the consequences, you must be tuned into what is happening for both yourself and others. Once you have read the situation, you can make choices—such as whether to tell a joke or not, whether to answer your cell phone or not, or when to voice your opinion...or not.

What to Do

Train yourself to read social situations. Ask yourself, "What is going on here? What are the interests, needs, feelings, and possible intentions of those involved?" Once you can answer these questions, you can choose behavior befitting the situation. An important aspect of assessing a situation is listening and paying attention. To choose appropriate behavior, pause for one second before responding to an impulse so your brain has a moment to choose your words or behavior carefully.

3.

We Are All Linked at the Brain

What to Think

Neuroscientists have discovered that our emotional states influence what others are feeling and thinking. This suggests a new way of looking at social interactions ranging from casual networking encounters to relations with those we love. We create beneficial emotional states in other people.

What to Do

First, be aware that your emotional state affects others. Being upbeat and positive creates positive emotions in others. Being negative and critical creates stress and discomfort in others. Work to be positive. Helping others feel good about themselves is an avenue to realizing your own goals. Also, be aware of others with whom you are in contact. If they are positive, they will help nurture you. If they are negative, they will bring you down. Choose to be with upbeat, positive people. You will be energized!

4.

When Stressed, We Become Vigilant

What to Think

When we are in situations where we have a higher level of anxiety, such as in networking situations, we become very attentive to the faces of people we interact with, searching for smiles of acceptance or frowns of rejection. This heightened awareness makes us more susceptible to feelings and fears of rejection, which may lead to a tendency to withdraw or hold back.

What to Do

Keep in mind that a mixture of acceptance and rejection is the norm in networking. You will meet people with whom you connect and others with whom you don't. Focus on the connections and consider the rejections part of the natural process of networking. Also, keep in mind that you can do a number of things (many of which are in this book) to increase your chances of connecting and reduce your anxiety.

5.

Aim for Empathy

What to Think

Empathy is how we understand another person's thoughts feelings, behaviors, and intentions. The greater our empathetic awareness, the easier it is to communicate and establish relationships with others. Empathy is greatly influenced by how much we focus on other people.

What to Do

People differ in their willingness and interest in paying attention to others. Those who are willing to put out the effort to pay attention have greater empathetic awareness and connect more easily with others. Make the effort. Pay attention to others by actively listening to and thinking about what they are saying. Look into their eyes and be conscious of what they are communicating through facial expressions and posture. Most of all, be aware that being self-focused kills empathy.

6.

Why Poker Players Wear Shades

What to Think

Our neural wiring transmits our every emotion to the 200 muscles of our face, making our feelings instantly visible. Displays of emotions are automatic and largely unconscious. Our brains are also wired to quickly and accurately read facial expressions. This is why even the best poker players wear sunglasses: to hide the muscles around their eyes and disguise their emotional reactions to the cards they have been dealt.

What to Do

Because you can't fake it, it is important to go into social situations with the right attitude and feelings. Your attitude and feelings will be far more positive when you feel confident about your networking skills, you feel confident about what you have to offer others, and have a genuine desire to meet and connect with others. When you have the right attitude, your face will tell others—and they will respond.

7.

It's About Rapport

What to Think

The primary goal of networking is to establish rapport. Rapport is a smooth, pleasant, and engaged sense of friendliness, where there are mutual feelings of warmth, understanding. and genuineness, all of which leads to trust. When we establish rapport with another person, we are more emotionally expressive, there is greater access to creativity, more efficient decision-making occurs, and there are greater levels of trust. You cannot create rapport with another person. You can only invite them to establish rapport with you and hope they respond.

What to Do

To foster rapport, be fully present with whom you are speaking. Being fully present consists of listening without thinking about what you want to say next, being aware of the other person's feelings, and not letting your attention be split. Also, communicate your positive feelings through what you say and your tone of voice. By communicating your attention and positive feelings, you let the other person know you are interested in building rapport with that person. If the person is also interested, he or she will accept your invitation.

8.

Don't Fake Rapport

What to Think

Some books suggest intentionally matching another person's posture, body language, tone of voice, and pace of speaking in order to establish rapport. Unfortunately, this comes off as fake, creates discomfort, and actually erects a barrier to even lower levels of connecting.

What to Do

If you do not feel a genuine connection with somebody, do not try to fake it. You can establish a level of social ease where you feel comfortable and networking is possible, but full rapport may not be achievable with that person. Do not assign a lot of significance to this; you can't establish rapport with everyone.

9.

Use the "Happy Face" Advantage

What to Think

The human brain prefers happy faces. People with happy expressions are less threatening and easier to approach.

What to Do

Smile more. When you are smiling, people see you as more approachable and are more likely to strike up a conversation with you. It also helps tremendously to actually be enjoying yourself and smiling because you feel good. The best feelings in networking situations come from being connected to others and enjoying good conversations.

10.

Laughter: The Shortest Distance Between Two Brains

What to Think

Research shows that even among complete strangers, a moment of playfulness or even outright silliness forms an instant connection. Laughing people feel a strong and immediate sense of closeness.

What to Do

Look for opportunities to display humor. Typically, it is best to focus the humor on yourself or the situation. Be sure to exercise caution with respect to risqué humor, as some people may be offended. Note that even telling a joke that falls flat can work if you are willing to acknowledge, humorously, how bad it was.

11.

Rejection Hurts, Really

What to Think

Our brains register social rejection in the same part of the brain that is activated when we are hurt physically. This is a holdover from the days when being a part of a tribe was essential for survival; exclusion or rejection was often a death sentence. Thus, the fear of rejection is similar to the fear of physical pain.

What to Do

Be aware that your brain is still wired for old tribal survival needs. When you start to experience the fear of rejection, tell yourself that it's the old brain wiring being activated. Rejection won't kill you; it does not even need to hurt. Assess the situation as it exists today. How important is it if a particular person is not interested in a relationship with you? It certainly doesn't have anything to do with your survival, even if it does feel that way!

12.

"It" Versus "You"

What to Think

Social relationships range from those based on simple respect and politeness to relationships based on affection and admiration. In simple respect-and-politeness relationships, people are often treated as an "it." They are seen as an end to a goal—"What can this person do for me?" In affection-and-admiration relationships, the goal is a truly supportive relationship in which individuals are treated as a "you." When we expect to be treated as "you," and are instead treated as "it," we feel terrible.

What to Do

Take the other person's perspective. See things from his or her point of view. As we do this, it becomes impossible to treat the other person as an "it." We may still want to achieve a specific goal with the person, but we do so with a deeper, more meaningful relationship, often with affection and admiration.

13.

First Impressions Are Just First Impressions

What to Think

Yes, it is true that at the first moment of meeting someone, we form an impression of that person. In fact, our brain registers an initial judgment, positive or negative, in just one-twentieth of a second. Our brain then spends another fraction of a second making judgments about what actions to take, given the situation. This does not happen just once, however; rather, it happens repeatedly during any social situation. Thus, our first impression is only that. It is subject to change, again and again.

What to Do

Our impressions of others form rapidly. Usually, we are left with only a vague sense of liking or not liking a person, without being aware of why. We then act on these feelings by either engaging in conversation with the person or avoiding him or her. This may result in our missing a valuable connection. To alter this pattern, tune into your reaction by paying attention to your initial impressions at a conscious level. Stay open and curious about the person. Don't let a vague sense stay vague. Figure out what you are reacting to in the other person. It may simply be that the person reminds you of a teacher you did not like. Don't let these old memories get in the way of good connections today.

14.

Use the Good Networker Profile

What to Think

There is a profile of a good networker. The profile consists of two elements:

- **Social awareness:** This consists of being sensitive to other's thoughts, feelings, behaviors, and intentions.

- **Social facility:** This is knowing what to do with the awareness in social situations.

What to Do

To improve your social awareness and social facility, work on the following:

- Understanding people's thoughts, feelings, and intentions

- Being good at dealing with people

- Gaining knowledge of rules and behaviors in social situations

- Learning to take the perspective of other people

- Being warm and caring

- Being open to new experiences, ideas, and values

15.

Tune In to the Situation

What to Think

Good networkers can read social situations and interpret the behaviors of others in those situations relative to their intentions, emotional states, and willingness to interact. This enables the good networker to know whom to approach, whom to avoid, and how to approach.

What to Do

You can develop situational awareness through observation and practice. If you are a beginner networker or are insecure about networking, spend time at networking meetings paying close attention to people in the room. Who looks open to being approached? Who is working the room successfully, meeting a lot of people? Who is spending most of their time alone? How do the good networkers stand, look, and act? How do the loners create their isolation? Take notes, look, and learn.

16.

Shyness Is What You Do, Not Who You Are

What to Think

Nobody is shy in every aspect of his or her life. Even the 30 percent of us who qualify as shy feel completely comfortable with family and friends. Shyness is defined as the tendency to feel awkward during social interactions, particularly with strangers. This awkwardness results in shy behavior, including difficulty talking with others, feelings of anxiety, averted gaze, hunched shoulders, avoidance of social situations, and limited networks. The good news is shyness is learned—meaning it can be *un*learned, too.

What to Do

Practice the behaviors of outgoing people. Learn a good handshake, practice small talk, and learn to be likeable and to be interested in others. Interestingly, some research shows that socializing online on sites like Facebook and LinkedIn helps some people to be less shy in the real world. It's worth a try!

17.

Networking: What's the Fear?

What to Think

Fear of networking occurs when we want to leave others with a positive impression of us but are doubtful that we can. When we meet other people, particularly strangers, we try to present ourselves as warm, cheerful, accomplished, successful, and competent. We want others to think we are smart and successful, but we fear that if we talk with them, they will get the impression we are not doing well in our careers and we are not very smart or competent. This results in fear, which is often displayed as shyness and avoidance of networking situations.

What to Do

Start by considering that this fear is based on what you imagine others are thinking of you, which may be totally wrong. Also, remember that other people are engaged in the same impression management. That means they are willing to support you to uphold your "public face" and will not embarrass you. Keeping these thoughts in mind will reduce your fear and enable you to become more comfortable and outgoing in a networking situation.

2

NETWORKING ATTITUDE: AUTHENTICITY AND POSITIVITY

18.
It's All About Attitude

What to Think

Good networking is about networking with the right attitude. You can learn all the right networking moves and strategies, but applying the moves without the right attitude will feel hollow and inauthentic both to you and to others. You will not get any joy just networking by the numbers.

What to Do

Learn, practice, and internalize the basic elements of the right attitude:

- Network to help others.

- Expect nothing in return.

- Focus on the relationship.

19.

Be Authentic

What to Think

Authenticity is the desire and ability to let yourself be real, not phony or contrived. It is being who you are rather than what you think others want you to be. Being authentic is how you connect with other people in a way that enables you to become worthy of their trust.

What to Do

Simply be yourself and let others get to know you. Do not focus on getting other's approval. If you are unhappy with certain aspects of yourself, work to change those characteristics rather than hiding them. Being inauthentic will be more damaging to a relationship than almost any negative trait you think you have.

20.

Networking Requires Us to Do Things We Don't Like

What to Think

Networking often requires that we speak with strangers and ask for help. For most people, these activities rank just below public speaking and going to the dentist on the discomfort scale. When we are faced with doing something uncomfortable and we are not absolutely forced to do it, we tend to procrastinate, avoid, and find easier tasks.

What to Do

The first step is simply paying attention to our discomfort and becoming aware of how it leads us to avoid or take the easier path. At a networking event, notice whether you are spending time with comfortable acquaintances rather than connecting with a stranger. Then take small steps to break out of your comfort zone. Talk to one person you don't know and see how it goes. Regardless of the outcome, pat yourself on the back for taking the risk. The more pats on the back you give yourself, the easier networking will become.

21.
You Need Other People

What to Think

Regardless of what you want to accomplish in life, you cannot get there alone. Apart from goals relating to your self-development such as exercising, you need others to help you reach your goals, whether they are business goals, relationship goals, or recognition goals.

What to Do

Establish the networks that will help you toward your goals. Find and establish relationships with like-minded individuals who share your visions and goals and, most importantly, share the awareness that it is easier to do it with others than alone.

22.

Even the Lone Ranger Had Tonto

What to Think

You have to do it yourself, but you don't have to do it alone. Although many of us don't realize it, human beings thrive on making connections and helping others. Still, lots of people believe that asking for help is a weakness.

What to Do

Redefine your belief. Instead of believing that asking for help is a weakness, think asking for help displays strength. Do not be blocked by feelings of vulnerability or fear of rejection. Networking is all about giving to get, and getting with the ongoing goal of giving.

23.

You Are Networking Constantly

What to Think

You may think networking only takes place when you are consciously trying to meet other people and find out about what they do and how they can help you. You may not be aware that you are constantly networking. In fact, networking is a common part of everyday life.

What to Do

Be aware of all the networking you do. Referring a neighbor to a good car mechanic is networking. Asking about a good place to eat is networking. Setting up a carpool is networking. Once you realize you are networking all the time, you can think of networking as easy and natural, and not so specialized and intimidating.

24.

Don't Keep Score

What to Think

Because networking involves give and take, there is a natural tendency to keep score. How much have I done for this person, and how much has he or she done for me? What has he or she done for me lately? Keeping score gets in the way of a healthy and productive networking attitude.

What to Do

Don't keep score. Remember that your networking success is based on the total return you get from all your networking efforts. Thus, in some networking relationships, it will be all give and no get. In other relationships, it will be all get and no give. In the long run, it will all equal out—with you being a winner. Also, if you maintain the right attitude, giving is its own reward.

25.

Networking Is About Helping Others

What to Think

Networking is about what you can offer others. Everyone has something to offer, whether it's a special skill or knowledge, introductions to others, time, or compassion. In order to be an effective networker, you should know what you have to offer.

What to Do

Be clear about what you have to offer. Each person you network with may need something different. The initial part of networking, after establishing a good solid connection, should be focused on what you can do to help the other person. It is important to ask the question, "How can I help you?" This question focuses on how you can help and will avoid your having to guess—maybe incorrectly.

26.

Important People Are Still People

What to Think

There will be times when you want to meet someone you consider an important person. They may be high up in an organization, rich, famous, or just plain important. It is natural to feel intimidated by such people and to be shy or hesitant to ask for something as valuable as their time, much less their help.

What to Do

Approaching these people is all a matter of attitude and being willing to take rejection. Like all other people, they will want to know the value of meeting you. You will need to persuade them that a meeting will be valuable. The problem is, you have little way of knowing what such a person will find to be valuable. He or she may be looking for something large, like a big business deal, or just looking to give back by helping someone in need. All you can do is ask. Be clear about what you are seeking and what you have to offer, and be ready to take no for an answer.

27.

Be Curious

What to Think

First and foremost, networking involves establishing relationships. The most useful mindset for establishing a relationship is that of curiosity. This involves being authentically curious about the other person—his or her thoughts, feelings, beliefs, life experiences, hopes, and aspirations.

What to Do

Approach every networking interaction with curiosity and an interest in genuinely connecting with the other person. Do not begin with a business agenda. If you have an agenda to make a sale, it is a sales call, not networking. Most people will respond warmly and positively to genuine curiosity.

28.

Everyone Has Something to Teach Us

What to Think

Each person we meet has something to teach us. Perhaps that something is about himself or herself; perhaps it's about the world; perhaps it's even about ourselves. We just have to listen. Entering a meeting focused on learning something helps us to be open and curious, and not totally focused on what we want.

What to Do

Listen for the learning and note it. Say something to yourself like, "I did not know that." Listen for new information about the other person, the world, and yourself. There is rarely a time when we cannot get more knowledge about the world and ourselves.

29.

Don't Be Surprised by Who Helps

What to Think

There will come a time in your life when you will have to reach out to people you know for help and support. Almost without a doubt, you will be surprised by the response you receive. Some people you were sure would support you will disappoint you. Other people who you did not think would help will be your biggest supporters.

What to Do

Recognize that this is the way of the world. Don't take it personally. Be forgiving. During a moment of need, it is a waste of energy to spend time being angry and resentful. If it is somebody close to you, tell that person your thoughts and feelings about how they are responding to you. It may be that you need to be more open about needing help and more specific about how they can help you.

30.

Don't Be Invested in the Outcome

What to Think

When you are invested in a specific outcome of a networking meeting, you will tend to force your agenda. When you are busy working your agenda, you will be focused on yourself, and you may miss another equally important outcome.

What to Do

Do not be emotionally tied to the goal that you set for a networking meeting. Keep your goal in mind, but don't think that if you fail to get what you want that the meeting was (or you were) a failure. You should have a goal, but be aware that if the goal is not realized, the meeting was still of value—although the value may not be immediately apparent.

31.
Network with Enthusiasm

What to Think

People are attracted to other people who are upbeat, energetic, optimistic, and enthusiastic.

What to Do

Put positive energy into networking. When you network in person, be positive and enthusiastic. Greet others warmly and genuinely with a firm handshake and an attitude of curiosity. When networking on the phone, stand up; it will help you put energy into your voice and communicate interest and enthusiasm.

32.

Be Positive

What to Think

People like to hear positive things. They tend to be wary of negative people and don't enjoy hearing negative things.

What to Do

Communicate positively as much as possible. Talk about what you want, not what you *don't* want. Focus on the positive aspects of even a negative situation. Find something good to say about every situation and person.

33.

Be Aware of What You Want from the Meeting

What to Think

It is helpful to be clear about what you want from a networking meeting. However, what you want should include relationship goals that can be accomplished in the meeting as well as your outcome goals for after the meeting.

What to Do

Before the meeting, review what you want to happen. Focus on earning the other person's trust, establishing rapport, and conveying to the other person your curiosity and willingness to be helpful. Naturally, you cannot make the other person feel these things, but it is helpful to have relationship goals in mind as well as outcome goals.

34.

Establish a Trusting Relationship

What to Think

People do business with and help people they know, like, and trust. Thus, effective networking is about establishing connected, trusting relationships that result in mutual aid.

What to Do

Focus on establishing a caring, trusting relationship. When networking, do not rush past the relationship building and "get down to business." Small talk is not just something you do to pass the time before you get to the important stuff. Small talk is the basis of relationship building. Get to know the other person. Let him or her get to know you, and relate at a personal level. Once you establish a good relationship, it will be easier to be mutually supportive and mutually beneficial.

35.
Network to Help Others

What to Think

Networking is most rewarding, both emotionally and productively, when it is in the service of helping others. A networking truism is that the more successful you are at helping others attain their goals, the more successful you will be at attaining yours.

What to Do

Focus on helping others achieve success. Keep thinking about what you can do to further others' goals. Who can you introduce them to that will result in their achieving both their professional and personal goals? Immediately upon meeting someone, think about whom you can introduce that person to; then make the connection.

36.

Don't Be Disappointed by Others

What to Think

Relatively few people are really good networkers. Most people know it is a good idea to network and many have learned the techniques. However, very few people fully embrace the notion that networking is about being committed to making others successful. These people will tend to disappoint you.

What to Do

Understand that being broadly committed to other people's success is an enlightened and evolved concept. Not many people are able to put themselves aside and truly focus on another's highest well being. The best you can do is display this quality yourself, and hope that others learn from your example. Most will, some will not.

37.

Networking Is a Process

What to Think

A networking relationship is an ongoing process of meetings, discussions, referrals, sharing of knowledge, and offering and receiving help.

What to Do

When first meeting someone, think long term. The first meeting is just the first step on a networking journey. Thus, don't try to accomplish everything in the first meeting. View the first meeting as an opportunity to build a trusting platform upon which further networking interactions will take place.

38.

In Networking You Can Trust

What to Think

Shy people are typically shy in social situations because they are busy avoiding other people's disapproval. Shyness indicates a lack of trust that other people will be caring and supportive in social interactions and not embarrass us. This lack of trust results in difficulty starting and maintaining conversations. However, in networking situations, everyone is interested in everyone else's success. You can trust their willingness to support you!

What to Do

Keep in mind that networking is a well-defined social interaction where good networkers are busy supporting each other in their goal of meeting other people and sharing information. Other networkers want you to be a good networker so their network gets stronger. You can trust networkers; they are out for your own good.

3

**BUILDING YOUR
NETWORK:
QUALITY, NOT
QUANTITY**

39.

Your Network Is Money in the Bank

What to Think

Your network is social capital in the same way your bank account and house are financial capital and your education is intellectual capital. The value of your network is based on the types and number of people you know, how closely connected you are to them, and how well your network is maintained. Arguably, your social capital is the most valuable asset you have. With good social capital, you can increase your financial capital and access intellectual capital.

What to Do

Treat your network as an asset to which you can contribute and that you can make grow. Keep an eye on its value. Have you been maintaining your connections through face-to-face meetings or on the phone? Have you been meeting new people? Have you been introducing people you know to each other? What has been the return on your social capital? Are you successful at getting the help and support you need from your network? You may find that your social capital needs investment. If so, start banking some connections today.

40.
It's Quality, Not Size

What to Think

Many people think that when it comes to personal networks, the more connections, the better. This is typically not true. Knowing many people does not mean you are networking effectively or that the people you know are people who will support your networking efforts. What really matters is where those connections lead to, and how they connect the otherwise unconnected.

What to Do

Analyze your network and consider whether you have networkers in your network. Your network needs to have people like you, who are interested in connecting and will support your networking efforts. If you find your network lacks networkers, seek them out by going to networking functions.

41.

Networks Need Diversity

What to Think

If your network consists of the same types of people, you will be limited in your access to important resources, including people and knowledge. The more diverse your network, the greater the chances you will find just the connection you need.

What to Do

Consider the people in your network. How similar are they in terms of their socioeconomic level, education, race, geography, profession, and politics? If your network is narrow in diversity, seek out people who will stretch its diversity. Consciously make an effort to meet and get to know new types of people.

42.

Be the Connection Between Groups

What to Think

If all the people in your network are connected to each other, it is a closed community—basically, a clique. What really matters is where your connections lead to and how they connect the otherwise unconnected. People who are connectors between groups are well-positioned to be innovators and influencers because they have access to ideas and information flowing in various groups. Connectors are in a position to combine different ideas and knowledge found in various groups into new products and services and to distribute ideas.

What to Do

Position yourself as the connector between groups. Connect your religious community with your neighborhood community or professional community by introducing people in the networks to one another. The more groups you connect, the more valuable you are as a networker, and the more valuable your network.

43.

It's Not Who You Know, It's Who Knows You

What to Think

The old saying used to be, "It's not what you know, it's who you know." In today's connected world, this has changed to, "It's not who you know, it's who knows you."

What to Do

These days, an important part of networking is putting yourself where you can be found by people looking for people like you. Typically, this is on easily found places on the Internet, including the numerous social networking sites such as Facebook and LinkedIn. In addition, there are dozens of strategies for getting yourself known. Write articles, blog, put up your own Web page, send e-mails to your network, etc. You don't have to start a major public-relations campaign. Just start small with something as simple as replying to a question someone has asked at a Web site you visit. People will read your reply, and you will be off and running.

44.

Everyone Is Only Three Networking Connections Away

What to Think

There was a famous study done in the 1970s that showed that there are only six degrees of separation between people. That means it only takes six handshakes to meet anyone with whom you want to connect. That study is outdated, however; now, there are only *three* degrees of separation between people.

What to Do

In the 1970s, it took as many as six steps to connect with someone because people did not know the most direct path to the person with whom they wanted to connect. With the Internet, it is now far easier to locate the shortest distance between you and the person you want to meet. Use the Internet to research the person. Learn about the person's prior jobs, where he or she went to school, and where he or she grew up. With his information, you can often discover the shortest path between you and your target contact. Also, the larger your network, the better your chances of quickly discovering a path to your target connection.

45.

Build and Maintain

What to Think

A good network, which you develop over a period of years, requires both building and maintaining.

What to Do

Focus on these two important tasks: meeting new people and keeping in touch with people you already know. One is no more important than the other. For the people you know, decide how often you will stay in touch with them; then connect with them on a regular basis with a meeting, a phone call, or an e-mail. For new people, stay active in going to new places and exposing yourself to new groups.

46.

Know the Right People

What to Think

Throughout life, people have a number of goals, both professional and personal. To achieve those goals, people need a
variety of contacts in various walks of life. For you to network
effectively, you need to be able to connect others with the
types of people they need as well as connect with those people yourself.

What to Do

Maintain relationships with people in different walks of life,
and connect those people with people you know who need
those contacts. Be sure you are connecting the right people
for the right reasons. This includes knowing what a person
needs and knowing what people have to offer. This can be as
simple as referring a friend with a leaking sink to a good
plumber or as complex as referring a friend who needs money
to a venture capitalist. Remember, maintaining connections
is equally important for what you will get as for whom you
can connect.

47.

Balance Takers and Givers

What to Think

There are many people in the world who will be happy to have you help them and will give nothing in return. These people are not wise in the ways and value of networking. You should help these people and not expect anything. However, it is important to balance your network with takers and givers.

What to Do

Make sure you network with skilled dedicated networkers. Networkers know the value of giving, and will be eager to find out from you how they can help you. By networking with good networkers, you will achieve a natural balance of giving and receiving.

48.

Know the Person You Are Referring

What to Think

When you meet someone, you may instantly think of a number of people to whom you can introduce that person, and you may be eager to make the introductions. However, your network is a valuable asset. You should be careful about whom you introduce to your trusted contacts.

What to Do

Take the time to get to know the person before making connections. Be sure you have a good sense of the person you are introducing. Is that person trustworthy? Is he or she a good networker? Will that person embarrass you? It may take several meetings before you feel confident enough to introduce the person to others in your network. Remember, a bad introduction may weaken a networking connection you have nurtured over a long period of time.

49.

Be Aware of Others' Motivations

What to Think

When networking, you will run into people who are totally focused on what they can get. They may be willing to give, but their giving is based solely on their calculation of what they will receive, either immediately or in the future.

What to Do

You may choose to spend time with these types of people. Just be aware that their motivation for spending time with you relates to how they can profit from doing so. Think of the interaction as a business transaction rather than networking.

50.

Be Specific About What You Need

What to Think

When networking, in order to receive help, you have to make it easy for others to help you. It is easier for others to help when they know specifically what you need.

What to Do

Be very clear and definite about how the person can help you. Before meeting, know what you want to ask for. If it is for help finding a job, be specific about the type of job you are looking for and the setting in which you want to work. If it is for business, be specific about your business request, whether it is for a sales referral or for access to capital. The more specific you are, the easier it is for the other person to provide the connections you need.

51.

Become Involved

What to Think

It is typically easier to meet someone and establish a relationship when you are involved in a common activity. The activity gives you a common focus and a way to relate to the other person.

What to Do

Don't just attend networking functions. Get actively involved with groups, learning activities, committees, or religious organizations. Even within networking groups, become involved with the running and organizing of the group. The more involved you are, the easier it will be for you to meet people and establish relationships.

52.

Share Knowledge to Get Knowledge

What to Think

In today's knowledge economy, knowledge is a valuable commodity. The more knowledge you have, the more valuable and marketable you are. In order to receive insider information, however, you will need to have information to share.

What to Do

Use your networks to constantly update your knowledge. Make sure your network includes people in the know—people who will share the latest trends, information, and privileged knowledge with you. Once you have information, share it generously and liberally—as appropriate, of course. The more information you share, the more information you will receive.

53.

Network Face to Face

What to Think

With today's online mass-communication technologies, it is easy to communicate with many people at once. But blogging, sending mass e-mails, and using social-networking sites does not take the place of connecting one on one with another person.

What to Do

Networking is about establishing connected, trusting relationships. Don't give up the blogs, the mass e-mails, and the online networking sites; just be aware that they are limited forms of networking. In order to truly network, you have to connect one on one, either in person or on the phone. So pick up the phone or make a date with those people with whom you want to start networking or maintain a networking relationship.

54.

Actively Connect People

What to Think

Connecting others is a primary activity of good networking. And the more connections you make, the stronger and more diverse your network will be.

What to Do

Don't wait to connect people. As soon as you see a good connection and you trust the people involved, make a call or send an e-mail. You may even want to make a call while you are meeting with one of the people. The longer you wait, the more likely you are to forget about making the connection.

55.

Receive as Graciously as You Give

What to Think

Networking is primarily about giving. However, networking becomes a balance of giving and receiving. It is important to receive graciously.

What to Do

Remember, the reward of your giving is the receiving of the help and support you need. You may be receiving from someone to whom you have given nothing. Receive that person's help or support graciously, knowing he or she is returning what you have graciously offered to others. Express your gratitude and reciprocate if possible.

56.

Ask for What You Need

What to Think

It may be easier for you to give than to ask for what you need. Asking involves all sorts of uncomfortable thoughts and feelings, like fear of rejection, vulnerability, and disappointment.

What to Do

Ask anyway! In networking situations, both parties know they are there to help each other. You are expected to ask for something. If you have established the right rapport and you are clear about your willingness to help others, asking for yourself is just a natural part of the process. If you are networking with a good networker, that person will respect and support your request for help.

57.

Network at Work

What to Think

Many people think networking is something they do outside of work, often in the service of getting more business or finding a job. However, studies show employees with better networks at work are promoted more quickly and receive pay raises more often. Your work network is important and should be managed carefully.

What to Do

Focus on your network at work. Who do you know? With whom do you have trusted relationships? How diverse is your work network? Apply networking attitudes, principles, and approaches on the job. Become involved in work projects not just for the work involved but also for the people with whom you will work. You may not see working on the holiday party as your highest career goal, but who will you meet, and how valuable will those people be to your work network? If you can extend your network, a seemingly inconsequential committee or project may be a networking goldmine.

58.

The Structure of Organizations Has Changed

What to Think

With downsizing, reduced layers of management, and automation of routine jobs, there is an increased interaction between companies to get jobs done that used to be handled entirely in-house. Thus, networks of relationships between organizations have become increasingly important.

What to Do

View your relationships with vendors, clients, industry colleagues, and the media as critical resources for doing your job well. Use all your networking strategies to build and maintain these relationships. Part of any networking strategy includes tracking and staying connected with people as they move from one company to another.

59.
Find Well-Connected People

What to Think

Some individuals have large, diverse, and well-maintained networks. These individuals are "hubs" for a number of networks and can access a variety of people quickly and effectively. Being connected to a hub is a very effective networking strategy.

What to Do

Identify people who are hubs and network with them. Hubs are excellent networkers. They are approached constantly by people looking to connect with them and their networks. Hubs are open to meeting with other good networkers and will contribute to the success of people in their network. Determine what you can offer, know what you would like to receive, and set up a meeting with a hub.

60.
Avoid Crisis Networking

What to Think

Many people think about their network only when they are in crisis, typically looking for a job. If a person only engages in crisis networking, that person will find that his or her network is weak and unsupportive.

What to Do

Be an "all the time" networker, constantly growing and nurturing your network. If a crisis emerges, your network will be ready, willing, and able to support you.

61.

Once Connected, Always Connected

What to Think

At any given time, certain people in a network will be active, and there will be ongoing communication. Other parts of the network will be dormant with no regular contact. However, a networking contact never gets disconnected through lack of contact.

What to Do

Many people feel hesitant to connect with old contacts with whom they have not spoken in a long time. However, you can reach out to any networking contact at any time, even if you have not communicated with that person in years. Typically, when you contact the person, you will be well-received, and he or she will be eager to catch up and help.

4

NETWORKING ETIQUETTE: BE RESPONSIBLE, RESPECTFUL, AND RESPONSIVE

62.

Treat Referrals with Respect

What to Think

When a person refers you to one of his or her contacts, it is a statement of generosity and trust. That person is being generous with his or her personal relationships, and is trusting that you will not embarrass him or her.

What to Do

Treat every referral with great respect. First and foremost, make a connection with the person to whom you were referred. Even if you don't follow through with a meeting, it is important to make the connection. Prepare for the meeting if appropriate, be on time, and send thank-you notes both to the person with whom you met and to the person who made the connection. Showing respect will identify you as a good networker and will result in more referrals.

63.

Make Your Meetings Convenient

What to Think

When you have requested a meeting, it is up to you to make the effort to set up the meeting and make the meeting as convenient as possible for the person with whom you are meeting. Even if the meeting will be mutually beneficial, it is good practice to play the host.

What to Do

Do not inconvenience your contact in any way. If you do not get the person on the phone, leave a message that you called and say you will call again to try to reach him or her. Do not leave a number and ask that person to call you. Once you contact the person, ask where it would be convenient for him or her to meet. Your contact is generously giving his or her time, so treat that time with courtesy and respect.

64.

Make the Connection, Then Get Out of the Way

What to Think

Connecting two people in your network is like setting up a blind date. You have a good sense that the two people have something in common and they would benefit from knowing each other. Once you make the introduction, however, the rest is up to them.

What to Do

As when you refer someone for a blind date, make the introduction, and then get out of the way. By making the introduction, you have done your part. It is not your responsibility to make the connection work. If the connection does not work, however, it is worthwhile for you to find out why so you have a better idea of the types of connections to make in the future.

65.

Keep Your Referral Source Informed

What to Think

Good networkers are constantly connecting people. They get positive feelings from introducing two people who are able to help to one another. When they refer you to someone, they are interested in how it works out.

What to Do

Keep your referral source informed. Let that person know when you have made the first contact. Tell him or her whether there will be a meeting. In the end, give that person some information about the outcome of the meeting. You do not have to provide great detail. A brief "We met, it went well, and I think we will be able to do some business together," is sufficient. A warm and profuse thank you is important as well.

66.

Reintroduce Yourself

What to Think

Often, we run into people we have met before, but they don't remember us. This has nothing to do with us; it has to do with the other person's memory. Do not take it personally.

What to Do

When you meet someone you know and that person does not seem to know you, or the person knows you but does not remember your name, simply reintroduce yourself. Tell the person where you have met before or how you know him or her. Taking the initiative to reintroduce yourself relieves the other person of embarrassment and demonstrates supportive caring. Conversely, if you do not know the person's name, apologize, admit that you've forgotten his or her name, ask what it is. Asking is far better than carrying on a conversation, constantly worried that you may have to use the person's name.

67.

Focus on the Event

What to Think

Every social event, presentation, and workshop you attend presents an opportunity to network. However, you are there for the activity first and networking second. Putting networking first communicates a lack of social awareness and an inappropriate focus on self-interest. For example, working the room during a funeral or a wedding is inappropriate, and will probably lose you any potential networking contacts.

What to Do

Focus on the event. If a significant networking opportunity presents itself, discreetly give a business card and arrange to follow up later.

68.

Guard Your Networking Reputation

What to Think

Networks are composed of connected people. Networks talk and communicate information quickly and effectively. When you are an active networker, your reputation is particularly well known. The bigger your network, the more widely your reputation is communicated.

What to Do

Guard your reputation very carefully. Be extremely careful to maintain integrity by not gossiping, by being true to your word, and by not misrepresenting yourself. The people with whom you network will quickly communicate how you treated them, your attitude, and the type of information you shared. The old adage, "If you can't say something nice about a person, don't say anything at all" is particularly important in networking. Also, if you promise to do something for a person, be sure to follow through.

69.
Use Your Relationships Judiciously

What to Think

There may be an individual with whom you have established a close relationship who, for one reason or another, is able to help a wide variety of people. Based on your close relationship, that person may find it difficult to say no when you refer someone to him or her. Making too many referrals is taking advantage of the relationship.

What to Do

Use good judgment when you refer people. Too many referrals become a burden on a person's time and good will. Make sure to check with the person about how he or she feels about the people you are referring and his or her availability to meet new people. Also, make a particular effort to give something of networking value to your special contact.

70.

Busy People Will Say No

What to Think

There will be times when you want to make a cold or blind contact with someone you want to meet. Connecting with these types of contacts is more difficult because you have not been referred and you must persuade them to meet with you. In addition, the person you want to meet is probably important and busy. Why else would you want to meet him or her?

What to Do

Make the call. Important and busy people guard their time closely and are very good at saying no. Thus, there is no opportunity for you to impose on them. If the person is interested in connecting, he or she will talk with you. If the person isn't interested in connecting, he or she won't. Your only risk is being rejected.

71.

Don't Be a Stalker

What to Think

Persistence and determination are admirable traits for a networker. However, there comes a point when these traits become annoying and aggravating for the recipient. If they think you're a pest, it is nearly impossible to recover.

What to Do

Contact the person a maximum of three times, utilizing at least two different methods of contact, such as phone and e-mail. After that, let time pass. Hopefully, an opportunity to meet will present itself. You may also want to try to locate someone who can open the door through a personal connection.

5

Networking Techniques: Network Like a Pro

72.

Outsource Your Networking

What to Think

Some people are highly motivated networkers. They love to network. They almost can't stop themselves. If you can connect with one of these driven networkers, they will network for you.

What to Do

Find networkers to "outsource" your networking. Connect with a couple of people who love to network and let them take the lead. They will love to introduce you to various people, particularly because it is part of growing and maintaining their own network. Just make sure you give them some direction about the types of people you are looking to meet and why.

73.

Forget the Golden Rule

What to Think

Everyone knows the Golden Rule: "Do unto others as you would have others do unto you." But following this rule may have you doing things to others that they would prefer you didn't do. The people with whom you are trying to connect may not share your preferences. Just because you like to network by getting together for a meal does not mean that all other networkers prefer to network the same way. Making assumptions about what another person would like and acting on those assumptions may cause that person to disconnect. Instead, change the rule to, "Do unto others as they would prefer to be done to."

What to Do

What to do is rather simple: Just ask about the other person's preferences. A question such as, "How do you prefer to follow up?" or, "Do you prefer to communicate by phone or e-mail?" will get you the answers you need about how to interact with that person. In turn, do not hesitate to state your preferences.

74.
Find a Role Model

What to Think

One of the best ways to learn how to do something is to observe a person who is good at the skill you want to acquire.

What to Do

When you are at a networking event or in a networking meeting, identify someone who is a skilled and polished networker. Make mental notes of the things that person does that attract others to him or her and help him or her make good connections. Look at how the person stands, what the person says, how the person looks, and how the person moves. Conversely, identify someone who is struggling to connect and observe what that person is doing or not doing. Choose one or two of the positive skills to practice at your next networking opportunity. After you master one skill or technique, move on to the next skill or technique. Before you know it, you will be the skilled and polished networker who others are observing.

75.

Prime Yourself for Good Networking

What to Think

Simply thinking of an action prepares the mind to perform it. Thus, we can prime ourselves for networking by reading about ideas that lead to good social interaction.

What to Do

Prepare a card that lists good social behaviors. These include the following:

- Listening
- Being polite
- Being curious
- Being open-minded
- Being outgoing
- Being bold
- Being courageous
- Having a good handshake

Read the card before networking to prime your brain to lead you in the right direction.

76.

Make a Good First Impression

What to Think

The saying goes, "You never get a second chance to make a first impression." Most, if not all, networking interactions start with a handshake. Your handshake should be a good one.

What to Do

Make your handshake firm, with two quick shakes. Your handshake should not be too hard or too soft. Also, you should maintain eye contact during the handshake. Here is a good trick to help with the eye-contact part: When shaking hands, look at the person's eyes and make a mental note of his or her eye color. To be really memorable, say something positive while doing so, such as "I really like your tie" or "Nice jacket." One good thing about a handshake is that it is easy to practice and perfect.

77.

Introduce People Correctly

What to Think

A critical part of networking is introducing people to each other. There will be occasions when you will want to introduce two people at a networking event or meeting. There is a proper way to make the introduction.

What to Do

A proper introduction is an elegant display of good style. It's proper to always introduce the lower-status person to the higher-status person. The introduction should be as follows: "Mr. CEO Jones, I would like to introduce Mr. Manager Smith. Mr. Manager Smith, I would like to introduce Mr. CEO Jones." When introducing peers, you can introduce either person first. In that case, you can use a brief introduction, such as "Tom Smith, this is Linda Hall." To help the people connect when you introduce them, you can include a piece of information that may be a conversation starter—for example, "Linda, Tom is a real-estate developer. As a realtor, I bet you have some interests in common."

78.

Make Yourself Likeable

What to Think

People are not born likeable or unlikable. Rather, people are likeable because of the things they do. You can increase how likeable you are by doing the right things.

What to Do

Likeable people do the following:

- Agree with others' opinions when they can and remain quiet when they can't.

- Give genuine compliments, even to people they don't know.

- Provide favors—for example, "I am getting more food. Can I get you something?"

- Disclose favorable information about themselves—for example, "I love to cook and my specialty is baking."

- Avoid or at least manage conflict. They help cool things down when people start arguing politics or religion or sports.

79.

Let Them Know You Are Listening

What to Think

Interestingly, it is fairly unusual to feel that we have been listened to and heard. We may get an impression that other people are listening to us because they are quiet and they are looking at us, but we often wonder whether they really heard us and understood what we were saying. When we feel both listened to and heard, we feel a greater connection to the person with whom we are speaking.

What to Do

Tell the person what you heard him or her say by reflecting. *Reflecting* consists of saying back to the person what he or she said. For example, you might say, "So what you are saying is that you think going ahead with the plan as it stands today won't get the results we want." After you have reflected what you heard, stop and let the other person affirm or correct what you said. Reflecting what a person says creates a higher level of listening and prevents you from tuning out by formulating what you want to say next. It also results in the other person feeling listened to and heard.

80.

Use Some Elegance to Keep in Touch

What to Think

It is easy and expedient to stay in touch via e-mail. Because it is so easy, however, it can lose significance. This is particularly true if you are connecting because of an important event such as a retirement, the birth of a child or grandchild, a major business success, or to say thank you.

What to Do

Write a handwritten note and mail it. Purchase some elegant, personalized stationery for letters and a nice box of thank-you notes. Also, get a box of informal or funny thank-you notes to send out for the right occasions, and send them liberally.

81.

When You Call, Be Prepared to Speak

What to Think

When you call someone to network and (hopefully) arrange a meeting, you may anticipate getting that person's voicemail. If so, you will be surprised when the person answers.

What to Do

Be prepared to have a conversation. To start the conversation, particularly if it is a first contact, it is very helpful to have prepared a script. The script should include a brief introduction, the reason you are calling, and a request for a meeting if appropriate. You can actually read the script over the phone, as the other person will not know you are reading a script. Try this with a friend; you will be surprised by how natural reading a script sounds.

82.

Any Reason Is a Good Reason to Connect

What to Think

Most people think they need a reason to connect with a contact. This is not true. Just calling a person to say hello is perfectly acceptable. However, if you are a person who needs a reason to call, any reason will do.

What to Do

Use any reason to make a call or send an e-mail. Track birthdays, send a holiday card, or send a note mentioning that you saw the person in an online article or that you heard the person presented at a conference. You can also reach out to people to tell them about some notable news about yourself: a change in jobs, a promotion, a new child or grandchild. Keep in mind your network likes to hear from you. With a little creativity, you can find a reason to connect with everyone in your network.

83.

Fly Solo

What to Think

Although it may be more uncomfortable to go to networking events alone, you will typically meet more people when you do so. It is easier for people to approach you if you are not in a group. Also, if you are alone, you will not be tempted to hang out with your friends. Remember, you are at the event to meet people, not to socialize with your friends.

What to Do

Either attend the event alone or, if you are with friends or business colleagues, circulate by yourself. A good technique is to look for people standing or sitting alone. These people may be nervous, and your reaching out to them will often endear you to them. Also, make sure to sit with people you do not know at a lunch or dinner. This gives you ample time to meet the new person and begin a relationship.

84.

Know the Nature of the Relationship

What to Think

Within networks, there are a variety of relationships from close friendships to distant acquaintanceships. When someone refers you to another person, it is important to know the nature of their relationship. If it is a close friendship, you will have little difficulty making a connection. If it is a distant acquaintanceship, your access may not be as easy.

What to Do

When you get a referral, always ask the nature of the relationship. By asking this question, you will know how close the relationship is and can then anticipate how easy it will be to connect with the person. You can accomplish this by simply asking, "What is the nature of your relationship with Mr. Smith?" You will also want to ask if you should wait for your contact to alert the person to whom you are being referred before contacting him or her yourself. Finally, ask whether it is the best to connect by phone or with an e-mail.

85.

At Networking Events, Meet a Lot of People

What to Think

When you are at a networking event, the goal is to meet as many people as possible. Thus, it is expected that you will not spend a long time with any one person. Networkers will not be offended when you move on to the next person.

What to Do

Spend only enough time with each person to get to know him or her sufficiently to decide whether a follow-up meeting would be of value. Once you have determined there is a connection, get a business card, let the person know you will contact him or her, and meet the next person. Be sure you make a graceful exit. Say something like, "It was good to meet you. There are so many people here I want to meet!" They will understand that you are there to meet others—they want to meet others too—and will accept a polite exit.

86.

Treat Business Cards with Respect

What to Think

A business card is a representation of who we are, our titles, our connections, our locations, and ways to contact us. Many people take great care to design a business card of which they can be proud.

What to Do

Treat all business cards with respect. When you are given a card, look at it. Perhaps comment on its look or notice where the person is from. If you are going to write on the card, ask permission first. Put the card away carefully. Don't just jam it in a pocket with little thought.

87.

Leave a Good Message

What to Think

During your networking activities, you will encounter situations when you will need to leave a voicemail message for a networking contact. It is important to leave a strong, coherent, pleasant-sounding message.

What to Do

Anticipate getting voicemail and script the message. Write the text of the message, and then read it into the voicemail. First, however, listen to how it will sound by calling your own voicemail and reading the message. As you listen to your message, make a note of any part of the text or the way you delivered the message you would like to change. Note that you can also read your script if you happen to get the person live. Listeners cannot tell the difference between a read script and a spontaneous statement.

88.
Who Do You Know Who...?

What to Think

There is a very easy way to ask people for the contact you need. It is simply using the phrase, "Who do you know who...?"

What to Do

Many networkers have tested this phrase, and it works. Do not alter the phrase. Use it every time you are asking for a contact or a referral. When I need to get my car fixed, I ask "Who do you know who...?" When I need to find a good tax lawyer, I ask "Who do you know who...?"

89.
Use Charisma

What to Think

Studies show that people are genuinely drawn to charismatic individuals. They are more willing to buy from them, to be influenced by them, and, most importantly for networking, to establish relationships with them. Although about 50 percent of charisma is innate, the other 50 percent is learned—which means anyone can train himself or herself to be charismatic.

What to Do

Charismatic people practice the following behaviors:

■ They assume every person they meet is important, and treat them as such.

■ They are genuinely interested in those around them. They ask them their opinions, inquire about their life and interests, listen, and don't interrupt.

■ They take the time to remember people's names and to use them in conversation.

■ They compliment people freely—as long as the compliments are sincere.

90.

Place Your Nametag Correctly

What to Think

Small things communicate how experienced a networker you are. Experienced networkers know where to place their nametags.

What to Do

As you shake hands, it is natural for the other person's eyes to travel down your arm to your right side. Placing your nametag on your right side makes it easy and natural for the other person to see your name. Also, make sure the writing is large enough to be read easily.

91.

Network Online

What to Think

Your networking efforts should be a combination of online and offline activities. There are a number of very robust and active online networking sites that you should make use of. Online networking is very efficient and can connect you to large number of people relatively quickly.

What to Do

Sign up and use sites like LinkedIn (http://www.linkedin.com), ZoomInfo (http://www.zoominfo.com), and Facebook (http://www.facebook.com). Similar to networking offline, invite others to network and connect others. However, do not become a numbers person, linking to as many people as possible without a goal or strategy in mind. Select contacts carefully. Keep your connections under 150 in number. Always keep a goal of meeting as many of your network contacts in the real world as possible.

92.

Get Organized

What to Think

Busy networkers start to accumulate contact information quickly. Many well-intentioned networkers let business cards stack up, and are then overwhelmed by the amount of work it takes to organize and enter the information into a system. In addition, they need to track who they know, where they met, and how long since the last contact. A stack of business cards with a rubber band around them just doesn't do the trick.

What to Do

Get a system today, preferably an electronic one. There are numerous contact databases, both online and offline, some expensive and some free. Examples include Microsoft Outlook and Google Docs. Choose a system and then use it. Be sure to enter contact information on a regular basis and set reminders when to re-connect.

93.
Don't Get Too Close Too Fast— or Too Slow

What to Think

Your goal in networking is to establish communication, respect, trust, and eventually a relationship with your contact. However, getting too close too fast will make you appear pushy. On the other end of the spectrum, moving too slowly will make you seem wimpy and uninterested. As the person gets to know you, he or she will drop his or her guard and invite you to get closer. Your job is to know when to hold back and when to move closer.

What to Do

Listen for clues to move closer. Does the person share personal information? Does the person ask for your opinion? Does the person share a joke? If so, what type of joke? Respond to the invitation to move closer by sharing your own personal information, giving your opinion, or telling a joke of the same type or cleaner (if you have a good one). You can also subtly invite a person to open up by sharing information about yourself. Just be careful it is not too personal or revealing, and don't push it if you get no response.

6

CREATING A
CONVERSATION:
TALKING POINTS

94.

What Is Your Name?

What to Think

At the beginning of a conversation, there is a brief window of opportunity to find out someone's name. If you miss the window, it is difficult to go back and ask a person their name. Even if you manage to do it, it will be awkward.

What to Do

Be sure to get a person's name right away. It is best to do this by introducing yourself first and then asking their name—for example, "Hello, I am Eric. It is nice to meet you. What is your name?"

95.
Be Relatable

What to Think

Many people find it challenging to make small talk. Small talk is easier when people know something about each other and can ask questions based on their knowledge.

What to Do

Be sure to give "free" information that others can relate to. Tell them where you are from, what you do, or your favorite activities. The more you self-disclose, the easier it is for others to think of something to say—and the more comfortable they will be speaking with you.

96.

Structure a Conversation That Works

What to Think

Many people struggle with small talk, which is the beginning of many conversations with strangers. Good networkers can draw others into a conversation. Broad categories of conversation include the following:

- **Setting talk.** This is a discussion about the present environment—the room, the weather, traffic, etc.

- **Topic talk.** This refers to conversation about broader issues.

Good conversationalists move quickly from setting talk to topic talk.

What to Do

Begin a conversation by introducing yourself. Engage in brief conversation about the environment (setting talk) and then move on by introducing topic talk. The good news is that when you're networking there are plenty of relevant topics from which to choose. At a networking event, you can always ask what led the other person to attend, what he or she thinks about the speaker, or what he or she does for a living. Caution: When you find yourself stuck on setting talk, the conversation is not going anywhere. Either change the topic or find another person to talk with.

97.
Don't Get Locked into Favorite Topics

What to Think

People who find small talk challenging tend to have a few favorite topics, such as sports or politics, that they use to start and maintain conversations. Although this technique may work occasionally, by using it you run the risk of not being able to engage enough people to be a truly effective networker.

What to Do

If you bring up a topic and it does not turn into a conversation, move on to another topic. To be able to do this, broaden your repertoire of topics. Read newspapers and magazines. Surf the Web. Also, being a good listener and being curious about the other person is a good way to maintain a conversation. What you learn from the current conversation can be good topics for a conversation with the next person you meet.

98.

In Casual Conversation, Knowing a Little Is a Lot

What to Think

When engaging in a conversation at a networking event, knowing a little about a variety of subjects works well. You do not have to be the world's foremost authority on a topic in order to speak about it. It does help, however, to know just enough to be aware of what others are talking about and to make a comment.

What to Do

Simply read a newspaper, watch a news show, or surf the Internet. Is there a major local or national news event people are likely to talk about? Has the local baseball team lost five in a row? What do the news outlets say people are concerned about or thinking about? You don't have to be an expert. Just have a little knowledge about a number of the most popular and current topics.

99.

Keep the Topic Relevant

What to Think

A important criterion for choosing a conversation topic is that the topic is relevant to both people. The topic must answer the question, "Why talk about that topic now, and with me?" If the topic is not relevant—"Why are you asking me about my home team, since I am not a sports fan?"—you run the risk of having the conversation fall flat.

What to Do

It helps to ask the other person a categorization question. A *categorization question* helps a person identify himself or herself in relation to a topic. Broad categorization questions are, "What do you do?" or "Where do you live?" The answers to these questions will help you land on a topic. Also, be sure to offer categorization information about yourself so the other person can offer topics.

100.

A Conversation Demands Talking and Listening; Do Both

What to Think

During a conversation, there are moments of transition during which one person stops talking and the next person begins talking. Transition points may be a moment of silence or a question. Good conversationalists provide opportunities for transitions to occur as well as take the opportunity to jump in when a transition point arises. Bad conversationalists either dominate the conversation or are silent when they could be talking.

What to Do

If you are speaking, provide transition opportunities by either pausing in what you are saying or asking a question. Be sure if you stop speaking to wait long enough for the other person to jump in. If you are listening, be sure to speak when an opportunity to talk presents itself or if the other person asks a question. It is perfectly okay to ask a question at a transition point if you don't have anything to say.

101.

Guide the Conversation

What to Think

As you engage in conversation, there will come a time when you'll want to shift the topic to something else. It could be that the topic under discussion is causing tempers to flare, is in poor taste, is silly, or is just plain boring. Whatever the reason, you can change the subject without being rude, or even obvious about it. In fact, if you shift away from a boring topic, you will make others happy.

What to Do

You can shift the conversation by taking the conversation down a slightly different path. For example, when someone is talking about his or her terrific grandchildren in detail, you can broaden the topic to parenting, empty-nest living, aging, etc. Another way to change the conversation is to just be straightforward and say, "I would like to change the subject." This works particularly well if things are getting tense. Just be sure to have another topic to switch to. It is particularly important to be able to switch the topic when the conversation has run its course and needs some new energy and direction.

102.
Disagree in an Agreeable Way

What to Think

There will come a time when you are conversing with someone with whom you want to maintain a relationship, but you disagree with what that person is saying. Often, you will be able to disagree silently and not feel like you are compromising yourself. Other times, however, you will feel compelled to make your thoughts and opinion heard.

What to Do

Start by keeping in mind that everyone is entitled to his or her thoughts and opinions. Then take this one step further and really try to understand the person's thinking from his or her point of view, not yours. If you still want to disagree, begin by acknowledging the other person's point of view, and then add yours—for example, "I understand how you could see it that way because of your background. However, I think...."

103.

When the Conversation Gets Bumpy, It's Time to Leave

What to Think

When a conversation is going well, there is a high degree of coordination between the speakers. Posture, timing, speaking pace, and even breathing are similar, and the speakers are often positioned close together. There is a meshing of movements, a smooth transition between speakers, and comfortable silences. As people reach the end of a conversation, they fall out of this smooth coordination, sending a signal that the conversation is about to end. If one of the speakers tries to continue the conversation at this point, it becomes uncomfortable and awkward.

What to Do

When the smooth conversation ends, move on. If it is a one-to-one meeting, it is time to end the meeting. If you are at a networking event, it is time to meet other people. You can end a conversation at a networking event by exchanging cards, agreeing to meet for breakfast or lunch, or by simply saying, "It was nice speaking with you but there are some other people I am hoping to speak with." Then move on.

7

Networking to Find a Job: Stay Positive

104.

Network for a Job with the Right Attitude

What to Think

People who are out of work and looking for a job often feel scared, depressed, and demoralized. In this state of mind, it is difficult to be a confident networker.

What to Do

Look for support from other job searchers, professional job-search coaches, and even a therapist if necessary. Go to job-search support groups and attend networking events. You will quickly see you are not alone. Other people are struggling, but lots of them are landing jobs.

105.

Networking for a Job
Is Networking

What to Think

During a job search, networking seems one-sided, with the job seeker needing help from his or her networking contacts. Even so, when you are networking to find a job, all the basic attitudes and strategies remain the same as in all other networking situations.

What to Do

Be sure to follow all the best practices, including thinking about how you can help people with whom you are networking. During a job search, your network often expands very quickly, so you will have more opportunities to connect people. Take the opportunity and become a better connector.

106.

Networking Is the Best Job-Search Strategy

What to Think

Every job-search expert, as well as industry research, confirms that networking is far and away the most productive job-search strategy. Unfortunately, for many job seekers, it is also the most difficult and stressful activity.

What to Do

Do not avoid networking. Take small steps to begin your networking efforts. Call close contacts and meet with them. Find a networking meeting to attend. Get yourself listed on networking sites on the Internet. Basically, just get in the game.

107.

Employers Like to Hire Referred People

What to Think

Most employers prefer to hire someone they know or a person referred by a personal contact or a current employee. In fact, many companies pay finder's fees to employees who refer someone who is hired.

What to Do

This strongly supports your networking strategy. Get your resumé to the hiring manager through a personal connection. When you see a job listing, the first thing to think is, "How can I get connected through my network to the hiring manager for this position?" You should be no more than three networking connections away from any hiring manger. Work your network.

108.

Know How You Can Affect the Bottom Line

What to Think

Employers want to know how your experiences will improve the company's well-being. Many people are poor job networkers because they fail to understand their high-impact skills, so they can't communicate how they can improve a company's bottom line.

What to Do

Know your strengths and how you benefit a company. Then develop a very brief summary of who you are and the value you bring. The summary should include a piece of enticing information that makes the other person curious about you and invites him or her to engage in a conversation. The information may be something you do that is unique or a significant accomplishment that communicates your skills and experience. The conversation may not take place immediately, but if the other person is curious enough, you can set up a meeting. This quick summary is effective at business networking events, social mixers—pretty much anywhere where you get the opportunity to market yourself.

109.

Everyone and Anyone May Be Your Next Connection

What to Think

When people are looking for jobs, they often overlook people they know but don't think of as part of their work world. When networking to find a job, every contact is a possible connection to a job opportunity.

What to Do

Tell everyone you know you are looking for a job. It could be a neighbor, a child's friend's parent, or even your hairdresser who will end up knowing just the person you should talk with.

110.

Make It Easy for People to Help with Your Job Search

What to Think

Letting people know you are looking for a job is a good start, but you need to give people guidance about how to help you. They need to know what kind of job you are looking for and what companies you would like to work for.

What to Do

Write a statement of exactly the type of job you are looking for—the job title, industry, and the job responsibilities. Put together a list of companies you want to work for and show it to networking contacts. You will be surprised how often someone will say, "I have a friend who works at one of your listed companies." Also, use networking meetings to find out about other companies that are not on your list but would fit well.

111.

Network Formally with Friends

What to Think

Many friends and acquaintances who are very willing to help are social connections. They do not know you in the world of work. Thus, they may not know what you do or the type of jobs you are looking for. Just saying you are looking for a job is not enough for them to know how to help you.

What to Do

Set up formal networking meetings with friends and acquaintances. Call them to set a breakfast or lunch meeting. Treat the meeting like any networking meeting. Tell them what you are looking for, share your list of target companies, and ask for referrals to people they know. Also, do not forget to network with your friend's significant others and family. They may have some surprise connections as well. And of course, as in all networking meetings, ask how you can help them.

112.

Getting Referrals Makes a Job-Search Meeting Successful

What to Think

Obviously, the best outcome of a job-search networking meeting is a connection to an open position. However, this outcome is rare. A more typical—though still valuable—outcome is referrals to new people with whom to network.

What to Do

Make getting new referrals a goal of a job-search networking meeting. Always ask the question, "Do you know other people I should be speaking with, and can you make the introduction?"

113.

Networking Is Easier if You Aren't Asking for a Job

What to Think

People are typically willing to meet with job seekers to help with their search. They are not willing to meet if they think they are going to be asked for a job and will have to say no. Asking for a job is a close-ended question; asking for help is a conversation starter.

What to Do

When you ask for a networking meeting, say openly and clearly you are not looking to that person for a job. You may need to say this more than once. Let them know you want to meet to find out information, review your list of target companies, and, if possible, be introduced to others who will also be good people with whom to network.

114.

Practice Networking Before Going After the Big Fish

What to Think

When you meet with contacts who are very valuable, influential, and well connected, you want to be at your best. If you have not been a consistent networker, your networking skills may need some development, however. Like any skill, your networking will get better with practice.

What to Do

Even though a big-fish contact may be able to accelerate your job search, wait to network with the big fish. Put together three to five easier, lower-risk networking meetings before setting up the big meeting. These first few meetings will give you an opportunity to learn what to say, how to answer questions, and how to follow through. The meetings may also give you some valuable information that you can share with the big fish.

115.

Networking Puts You in the Driver's Seat

What to Think

When you send your resumé to a company or you are waiting for a recruiter to call, you are in a passive position. Passivity in a job search leaves you feeling out of control and helpless. Networking is an active strategy and can be as productive as your time, energy, and commitment allows.

What to Do

Establish an active networking process. Combine attending networking activities with one-to-one networking meetings and sending out networking letters. An active networking process will have you fully engaged in a productive job search.

116.
Stay in Control of the Process

What to Think

During job-search networking, you will meet people who will offer to pass on your resumé or to contact someone on your behalf. They have the best intentions and may follow through, but it is on their timeframe and based on their list of priorities.

What to Do

Always find out the names of the people to whom your contact will be sending your resumé or calling on your behalf. Suggest that you can follow through with these people directly, but do not push too hard if your contact prefers to make the connection first. Establish a timeframe by asking when you can contact the people to whom he or she is referring you. This will set a deadline and move this activity up on his or her priority list.

117.

Keep the Connection Going

What to Think

Many people are very busy networking during a job search and let their network go back to sleep once they land a job.

What to Do

Keep your job-search network awake. When you land a job, be sure to inform everyone you networked with during your job search. Make networking part of your regular work activities and keep attending any networking groups you connected with during your job search.

118.

Selling Yourself Is the Hardest Sale of All

What to Think

Many people feel comfortable networking for business because it focuses on a service or product other than oneself. As long as we're acting "on behalf" of the company or in the best interests of someone else, we find the courage to do great things. But ask us to act on our own behalf, and even the most seasoned salespeople lose confidence.

What to Do

Give yourself a break. Just be aware that networking (selling yourself) during a job search is a very difficult task for even the most confident, outgoing people. Expect to be nervous, to fear rejection, and to have difficulty assessing yourself accurately. Start with small steps; seek help from friends, contacts, and professionals if necessary.

119.

You Often Get the Most from People You Know the Least

What to Think

You are more likely to get new information or access to new opportunities from people with whom you don't have close ties. Many people find new jobs from their weaker ties—their acquaintances—and not their strong ties—their friends and close associates.

What to Do

Continue to network with the people you know the best. However, have the goal of encouraging them to introduce you to the people who they know but you do not. Also, focus on networking with people with whom you are an acquaintance, not a close friend.

120.

Use a Presentation to Network

What to Think

It may be difficult for the person with whom you are networking to remember your target companies, skills, strengths, experience, and desired positions. Giving a resumé is too formal. Besides, it is a historical document rather than a forward-looking document.

What to Do

Put together a brief printed presentation to use during networking meetings. Include the following information in the presentation:

- The areas within which you can contribute to a company (for example, in marketing or product development)

- Target job titles

- The types of companies you want to work with (size, geography, revenue, culture etc.)

- Some noteworthy accomplishments about which you can tell stories

- Specific companies for whom you want to work

- Specific benefits you can provide to a company (basically, why a company should hire you)

Use the presentation as a guide during your conversation and then give your contact a copy.